How We Got the Bible

and

Why You Can Trust It

How We Got the Bible

and

Why You Can Trust It

Mike Taliaferro

Illumination Publishers International

How We Got the Bible and Why You Can Trust It

ISBN: 978-0-9824085-2-0

Unless otherwise indicated, all Scripture references are from the Holy Bible, New International Version, copyright 1973, 1978, 1984 by the International Bible Society. Used by permission of Zondervan Bible Publishers.

Cover and book interior design: Toney C. Mulhollan

www.ipibooks.com

Illumination Publishers International
www.ipibooks.com
6010 Pinecreek Ridge Court
Spring, Texas 77379-2513

Dedicated with love and respect to

Disciples of the
Mission Point Christian Church
San Antonio, Texas

Contents

FOREWORD

You will find this small book, *How We Got the Bible and Why You Can Trust It*, truly captivating. It answers questions, boosts faith, silences criticism, and thoroughly enthralls anyone earnestly seeking reasons to believe. The virtue of the book lies in its compactness—which is the result of brevity (sure to be appreciated by many readers) combined with punch.

I heartily recommend it, and am confident that you will be thrilled even as you are educated. Read it and share it with your friends. Revel in the fact that the Christian faith is utterly consistent, compelling and trustworthy.

Dr. Douglas Jacoby
Marietta, Georgia

INTRODUCTION

The Bible has been under heavy attack for the last two centuries. Scholars and professors have assailed the manuscripts as unreliable, the authors as inaccurate, and the characters of the Bible as mythical figures. To liberal scholars, King David was a fireside legend. Moses was an illiterate wanderer. A few even say Jesus never lived. Others claim that the story of Jesus was written hundreds of years after the events actually took place. Today some still teach that the Bible is a hopeless hash of traditions handed down through the centuries, a weak historical document whose value is somewhere between Aesop's fables and Greek mythology. Professors from the late 1700s and 1800s pounded away at the Bible's alleged problems as an historical document. They berated the Scriptures for being written far too late to be a reliable record of actual events. The critics had the hammer raised over the last few nails in the Bible's coffin.

Chief among the critics was the German writer F. C. Bauer, who along with several other theologians, relentlessly disparaged the reliability of the Scriptures. Believing the New Testament to have been written close to the year 200 A.D., these theologians surmised that it was impossible for the New Testament to be anything other than myth.

Although their theories still surface from time to time, they have been shown conclusively to be wrong— dead wrong. History, archaeology, and advances in the study of the manuscript record have beaten back these attacks. It is now clear that the Bible is accurate historically. It is accurate culturally. The manuscripts give us the genuine words of the authors. There has been virtually no corruption of the text. The rubble has been cleared and the Bible is still standing tall. Whether you personally believe the book is your decision. But the Bible is the accurate record of the accounts of the prophets and the testimony of the apostles. Only the most biased critics would deny that today.

So often I speak with believers who do not realize the depth of evidence that substantiates the Scriptures. Students, parents, and other Bible readers don't realize how much positive evidence exists. In the following pages, not only are we going to explore how we got the Bible, but we are also going to see just how trustworthy it is. I think you will be amazed at the mountain of evidence and research validating the Scriptures. I know your faith will be strengthened. Quietly, and without much fanfare, the

Bible has proven itself to be far stronger than any of its critics had conjectured.

Without a doubt, it is the greatest book ever written. Consider these facts:

• The Bible was written over a span of 1500 years (circa1400 B.C. to 80 A.D.), across 40 generations.

• It was written on three different continents, in three languages (Hebrew, Aramaic, and Greek).

• Fifty writers from every walk of life, including kings, peasants, philosophers, fishermen, statesmen, and scholars contributed to the Scriptures.

• It contains hundreds of prophecies fulfilled through the centuries.

• It is reliable both historically and culturally.

• All these writers, across all those centuries, stand united with one message. In regards to topics such as truth, purpose, mission, God, man, reality, sin, righteousness, origin, and destiny, the Bible is totally unified. Just try getting fifty religious leaders in your city to agree on any of the aforementioned topics!

• Matters of science are dealt with simply and forthrightly, devoid of absurdities. (Compare to the Babylonian story of creation, which contends that the earth was formed from body parts of one of the gods after a fight broke out in heaven.)

• At one time the ancients thought there were about

1100 stars in total. In 600 B.C., Jeremiah (33:22) described the stars as "uncountable"—long before the Hubble telescope demonstrated it. The dimensions of Noah's ark are also interesting. Measuring 300 x 50 x 30 cubits, the ark uses the same paramenters as engineers use for most seagoing vessels today. How did they know?

• The United Bible Society alone sells and distributes over 110,000 copies of the Scriptures every day. The Bible is the most printed book in history.

• Currently, at least a portion of the translated Scriptures exists in more than two thousand languages, spoken by over ninety percent of the world's population. Translation of the Bible continues in more than a thousand languages, and even in those languages where it has long been in existence, new translations continue to be made.

• The Bible has better manuscript evidence than any other ten ancient works combined. It is better attested than even the works of Shakespeare.

• Voltaire, the French atheist who died in 1778, said Christianity would pass away within a hundred years. It was Voltaire who passed away; Christianity flourished. Within fifty years the Geneva Bible Society was using his house to print and distribute Bibles!

I know, I know. All of this doesn't prove the Bible is the word of God, but it does prove that the Bible is unique among all books. It certainly deserves your attention. ☙

Isn't Jesus a Myth?

Let's begin with the rumor that Jesus is not even a real historical figure. The distorted assumption is still making the rounds that Jesus was a myth, sort of like a Robin Hood or Santa Claus. Some cling to the old story that Jesus was an invention of later writers and that he never lived at all. Although this theory is patently false, let us quickly address it.

Please note that it is hard to find a scholar today who seriously proposes that Jesus was not a true historical figure. Virtually everyone recognizes that a man named Jesus lived 2000 years ago in Palestine.

H. G. Wells, an atheist, wrote of Jesus in his book, *Outline of History*, "One is obliged to say, 'Here was a man. This part of the tale could not have been invented.'"[1]

Will Durant is a former professor of philosophy and history at Columbia University. He spent two chapters in *Ceasar and Christ*, Volume 3 of *The Story of Our Civilization* depicting Jesus as a historical figure right along with the Caesars and Alexander the Great.[2]

The Encyclopedia Britannica uses over 20,000 words to describe Jesus. That is more than Aristotle, Cicero, Alexander, Julius Caesar, Buddha, Confucius, Mohammed or Napoleon.

There is more than sufficient evidence to have convinced these and many other scholars that Jesus actually lived. What is that evidence? It comes from the many non-Christian writings of the period.

The Samaritan historian Thallus wrote as early as 52 A.D. about Christ. Writing to give a natural explanation for the darkness that occurred on the day of the crucifixion, Thallus discussed Jesus and his death. The passage on Jesus was contained in Thallus' work on the Eastern Mediterranean world from the Trojan War to 52 A.D.[3] Interestingly, Thallus tried to explain away the darkness at the crucifixion as being an eclipse. It is important to note that Thallus did not debate the universal darkness experienced that day. That point he accepted. He only tried to explain the darkness away. He confirms Jesus as a real historical figure.

Cornelius Tacitus was a Roman historian who wrote

in the year 112 A.D. He discusses Jesus in his historical work, *The Annals of Imperial Rome.*[4] Noting Nero and his persecution of the believers, Tacitus mentions both Christians, who were burned alive at the stake, as well as Christ himself. Tacitus tells us that "Christus" (Latin for Christ) was the origin of the name Christian and that Christ had been executed by Pontius Pilatus (Pilate).

Gaius Suetonius Tranquillas, chief secretary of Emperor Hadrian, also wrote about Jesus. In 120 A.D. he noted, "Because the Jews at Rome caused continuous disturbances at the instigation of Chrestus, he expelled them from the City."[5] Chrestus is a variant spelling of Christ. Apparently Suetonius is referring to riots that broke out in the Jewish community in Rome during the year 49 A.D., as a result of which the Jews were banished from the city.

Jewish historian Flavius Josephus became the court historian for Emperor Vespasian in approximately 72 A.D. He mentions Jesus, Pilate, the crucifixion, and Jesus' claims of being the Messiah.[6] Josephus died in 97 A.D.

There are other references. A personal letter by a man named Mara-Serapion to his son in 73 A.D. mentions Jesus.[7] Pliny the Younger, the governor of Bithynia in Asia Minor in 112 A.D., wrote to the emperor Trajan about Christians and their devotion to Christ.[8] The Talmud mentions Jesus several times.[9] Lucian, the Greek satirist, poked fun of Jesus and Christians about 170 A.D.[10] All of these are non-Christian sources. This list doesn't include the many thousands of references to Jesus found in historical documents by Christian writers.

There is no doubt about the historical existence of Jesus. He lived in Palestine. He created quite a stir. Thousands of people were affected by his life. Anyone is free to say they don't believe in him as Lord. No serious historian, however, would propose that he is a myth or legend. He is every bit a figure of history as Abraham Lincoln or Mahatma Gandhi. ಠ

CHAPTER TWO

Old and New Testament Background: What the Critics Are Saying

Having established the existence of Jesus as a historical figure, we must now examine how reliable the Bible is as a witness to his life. How accurate are the Scriptures? Can we trust what they say? Many people today, when asked why they believe in Jesus, reply something along the lines of, "Because of the miracles he did." They might mention fulfilled prophecies, the fact that he rose from the dead, or how he has radically changed their lives.

But where does one learn about these things? Be it his miracles, the fulfilled prophesies, or his resurrection, our primary source of information is the New Testament.

If the New Testament can be discredited, then believers are on shaky ground. Indeed, this was the point of attack for many of the Bible's critics over a century ago. Claiming that the New Testament was written about 150 to 200 years after the death of Jesus, some writers asserted that therefore it was impossible to trust the Bible. It was not an eyewitness account they claimed, because it was written so much later than the actual events. In other words, they asserted that the New Testament was a forgery. They believe that oral traditions became confused and mixed in with half-truths and wishful thinking. How could anyone hope to untangle the mess? Some people even wondered if unscrupulous monks in the Dark Ages could have added in a few choice miracles to enhance the life of Jesus.

Disciples need not fret. This argument is more than fifty years out of date. We'll confront it in a moment.

A second question must be addressed. Even if we can show that the Scriptures were written in the middle of the first century as they claim, how reliable are the manuscripts we have? What if it were shown that the manuscript evidence is very scarce, and perhaps a thousand years removed from the original documents? Then our faith in Jesus would be based upon an unreliable document. It is true that we would be skating on thin ice if our earliest manuscript dated from, say, 1000 A.D. A significant amount of corruption can take place over a thousand-year period, even if the copyists were careful.

This theory is exactly what many scholars postulated at the beginning of the twentieth century. Some still raise these points today. They try to paint the New Testament as a later document. They also attack the manuscripts as corrupted and unreliable. Strange as it may seem, much of this teaching was actually done in the divinity schools of some of the large American and European universities. You may have heard these points yourself. These attacks took their toll and some needlessly lost their faith. The New Testament is an important part of our Christian witness. It is the eyewitness accounts.

A "blind faith" may seem adequate for some, but most of us would be very encouraged to have some concrete answers. And we'd like to share those answers with others. Fortunately, there is a mountain of evidence that supports the Bible as a reliable, historical document. Archaeological finds and a wealth of new textual evidence from the last 150 years have silenced the cries of the critics. It is a fascinating story. So let's back up a bit and begin with some background.

Background Information

While skeptics of the Bible had said there was no alphabetic writing at the time of Moses (1400 B.C.), the truth turned out to be quite different. Archaeologists have discovered alphabetic writing in Egypt dating back 400 years before Moses was born. Archaeology has also shown us that the Sumerians were writing more than 2000 years before Moses lived. The Egyptians were developing hieroglyphs as early as 3000 B.C. We also have letters written during the time Moses lived, correspondence between governors of cities in Palestine and the Egyptians. Having grown up in Pharaoh's court, Moses was undoubtedly quite literate.

The ancients wrote on a variety of materials. There are stone inscriptions surviving from many different cultures. At the Behistun complex in Iran, for instance, is a monument to King Darius carved into the side of a limestone mountain around 500 B.C. Larger than the sculptures on Mount Rushmore, the complex includes an inscription in three languages: Akkadian, Elamite, and Babylonian cuneiform, in which such Biblical figures as Darius and Xerxes are mentioned. Xerxes was the husband of Esther, whom we know well from the Old Testament. It is an exciting example of how archaeology has confirmed the reality of numerous people, places and cultural details mentioned in the Scriptures.

The ancients also kept records on clay tablets. Excavation of the library of the palace archives of the Ebla Kingdom in modern-day Syria uncovered more than 17,000 clay tablets dating from before Ebla was destroyed in 2200 B.C. The Ebla library mentions many Old Testament cities and confirms the existence of thriving trade between Ebla and some cities of the plain, possibly including Sodom and Gomorrah. Other great libraries of clay tablets have been found, which along with the tablets from Ebla, shed light on ancient cultures and confirm the validity of the social customs we read of in the Old Testament.[11]

Wood and pottery were also used for record keeping. Pottery scraps were often used for notes and receipts. Paper was not introduced until much later, due to papermaking technology being a secret guarded closely for centuries after its invention in China in the second century A.D.

The Old Testament texts were written and handed down on specially prepared animal skin called parchment or vellum. The Jews had specific regulations and traditions for the preparation of these skins and the copying of the Scriptures onto them. These fine skins provide a superior surface for writing and are very durable, as the text has been preserved for thousands of years on them.

Papyrus is a paper-like substance in use throughout the Mediterranean as far back as the third millennium B.C. and continuing to the present day. Papyrus is made from a reed plant (grown predominatly in the swamps of the Nile River) that reaches 12 to 15 feet in height, with hollow stalks as thick as a man's wrist. The reed is split, softened and pounded flat to make sheets, which can be joined to make longer sheets. Papyrus was the predominant medium for the making of books in ancient Greece and Rome. Short documents appeared in page form. Longer documents would be glued end to end and rolled up in a scroll. A papyrus roll was limited to about 30 feet in length; beyond that it became unwieldy. The New Testament books of Luke and Acts were probably split for that reason. If kept together, they would have been too long for the scroll format.

About the time of Christ, the scroll format gave way to the codex or book form. A codex was simply a stack of papyri, with a binding on the edge. It contained more writing space, and was easier to use and transport. Christians seemed to prefer the codex form, while the Jews preferred to use scrolls in the centuries after Christ.

Papyrus documents are fragile, and only survive well when stored in a protective environment such as a sealed tomb or jar in a very dry climate. The majority of ancient papyri that survive today were recovered in Egypt.

The New Testament documents were probably written down originally on papyrus. As careful as the early Christians were with the documents, eventually they perished with use. No originals (autographs) survive. During the third century A.D., the far more durable vellum codex became the popular form for the New Testament texts. The early churches archived their copies of the apostles' writings using vellum. Our two most valuable New Testament manuscripts in existence today are written on high quality vellum from about 325 A.D.

The Bible was written in three different languages: Hebrew, Aramaic, and Greek. Almost the entire Old Testament was written in Hebrew, which is written from right to left and Hebrew is still spoken today in Israel.

A language similar to Hebrew, Aramaic became the language of the common man in Palestine after the time of the exile (500 B.C.). Six chapters in Daniel, along with four chapters in Ezra, are in Aramaic. Also, phrases in the New Testament like "Abba", "maranatha", and "Eli, Eli, lama sabachthani" are in Aramaic. A form of Aramaic is still spoken in and around Damascus, Syria.

Virtually the entire New Testament was written in Greek. Thanks to the military conquest by Alexander the Great, it was the universal language of the day. The common man's Greek of the first century was called *Koine* Greek. It had its own style and peculiarities that were unique to the first century. Greek, of course, is still spoken by millions of people today. The letters of the Greek alphabet are the same, though the vocabulary of the Greek language has evolved. Many words, however, are the same; Greek has changed less in the last 2000 years than English has changed in the last 500 years. In my Biblical Greek class at university, the professor would sometimes ask the students from Greece to read the text aloud. Although the pronunciation today is almost certainly different than during the time of the apostles, it was fascinating to hear it read. ❦

How Accurate is the New Testament?

As previously mentioned, when judging the accuracy of any ancient text, two questions are extremely vital. First, how long is the time span between the events themselves and when they were finally written down? If the time span is long, say, over a thousand years, then there is a greater chance the events have been corrupted or embellished. The tenets of Buddhism, for example, were written down about five hundred years after Buddha lived. The Hindu Vedas were written down a full seven hundred years later. Most would ask, "How could an ancient author accurately report the events of several centuries before him?" In contrast to these religious texts, the New Testament claims to be written by participants and eyewitnesses. It places itself squarely in the events of the first century.

Second, how long is the time span between the original autographs and our earliest copies? If the text was written early, but our earliest copy is a thousand years later, then obviously there could be corruption in the text.

Fortunately, the New Testament passes both these tests with flying colors, unlike most books of antiquity.

Written during or immediately after the events

Most of the events of the New Testament occur between the years 27 and 62 A.D. The ministry of Jesus begins in 27 A.D., and the book of Acts ends with the apostle Paul in prison about the year 62 A.D. How long after 62 did they start writing down the books? A hundred years? Two hundred years, as some scholars guessed? Surprisingly, the first book of the New Testament to be written was Galatians, penned by the apostle Paul in 45 A.D. That's right, only fifteen years after the death, burial, and resurrection of Christ, the church is beginning to record its history and doctrine. When Paul wrote Galatians, the events of the book of Acts were still very much in progress. Paul wasn't recording oral tradition from centuries gone by. Instead, he was reporting as a participant and an eyewitness. Much of the New Testament was written *as the events were taking place!*

The other books followed Galatians quite quickly. While the events of the New Testament closed for the most part by 62 A.D., [12] scholars now believe that the documents were completed by the year 69 A.D. [13] That means that only a seven-year gap exists between the events that the New Testament describe, and the completion of the Scriptures. That's a tiny gap, historically speaking. As you'll see in a moment, a time span that short is viewed by historians as negligible and insignificant. The writers were obviously in a great position to report accurately the events they had witnessed. They were not recording oral tradition handed down from their great-great-grandparents, as some have proposed. They were eyewitnesses writing about what they had seen and heard.

Dr. John A. T. Robinson, in his 1976 book, *Redating the New Testament*, concluded that *all* of the books of the New Testament were written prior to 70 A.D.[14] William F. Albright, one of the great biblical archaeologists from the first half of the 20th century, wrote, "We can already say emphatically that there is no longer any solid basis for dating any book of the New Testament after about A.D. 80, two full generations before the date between 130 and 150 given by the more radical New Testament critics of today."[15] He later was quoted in the magazine *Christianity Today* as saying, "In my opinion, every book of the New Testament was written by a baptized Jew between the forties and the eighties of the first century A.D. (very probably sometime between A.D. 50 and 75)."[16]

In terms of time spans, there is no doubt about it. The period of time between the events and the writing is extremely short. The first New Testament book was written only 15 years after the crucifixion of Jesus, and during the events of the book of Acts. The book of Acts was completed only seven years after the final events recorded in Acts (Paul awaiting trial). Indeed, it appears that almost the entire New Testament was completed before Jerusalem was sacked by the Romans in 70 A.D.

What is the importance of these facts? First of all, the old argument that the Bible is a collection of stories written down centuries after the death of Christ is an indefensible argument. The New Testament is a first-century document.

Second, the accuracy of the text is powerfully validated. Scholars have realized that the time span between the events and the writing is far too short a time for myth and legend to have crept into the text. There is no way that the apostles could have gotten away with wild lies. The participants and witnesses were still alive. Critical non-believers were still alive. The New Testament was circulated in the cities where all these people had lived. The various churches endorsed the books of the New Testament as valid. There was simply no way that fantasy and falsehoods could be introduced into the text while so many hundreds of eyewitnesses were still alive.

In much the same way today, if I told you Nelson Mandela was released from prison in South Africa in

1990, you would agree. If I said he died and rose from the dead, you would laugh. We are all too close to the events. As I edit this text in 2009, it has only been nineteen years. Memories are fresh. We are too close in time to the events to start inventing wild rumors and lies. Hundreds of eyewitnesses are familiar with the story, just as when the apostles were testifying to what they had witnessed. Knowing that the New Testament is from the first century gives us confidence that the story it tells is accurate.

What about the "originals"?

Here one might inquire, "Why don't we have an original or "autograph?" As stated above, the original papyrus texts would have eventually worn out, much like our paper Bibles wear out today from continued use. Still, it appears that the originals lasted a long time. The churches treasured the autographs and apparently had many years to transcribe and distribute copies. Some scholars feel that the autographs were in existence for at least a hundred years in the libraries of the first-century churches. I love this fascinating quote by Tertullian in 196 A.D., written, scholars believe, while the original letters of the apostles were still in existence:

If you are willing to exercise your curiosity profitably in the business of your salvation, visit the Apostolic churches in which the very chairs of the

Apostles still preside in their places; in which their very authentic Epistles are read, sounding forth the voice and representing the countenance of each of them. Is Achaia near you? You have Corinth. If you are not far from Macedonia, you have Philippi and Thessalonica. If you can go to Asia, you have Ephesus. If you are near Italy, you have Rome.[17]

It appears that the church had plenty of time to make numerous copies of the original texts. Thousands of these copies survive.

Although we don't have the original autographs of the New Testament (or of Plato or Homer or any other ancient work), we can be very confident that we have the authentic text accurately transmitted. The letters were written, received, copied, circulated (Colossians 4:16), publicly read (1 Thessalonians 5:27), and archived by the early church. Our earliest copy dates all the way back to about 110 A.D. (Papyrus #52 currently in Manchester, England). Some scholars date it as older, but 110 A.D. is a realistic estimate. It is astonishing that we can read a papyrus copy of a portion of the gospel of John. It may well have been a first-generation copy. How does papyrus #52 read compared to our Bible today? Virtually the same![18] The discoveries of the papyrus texts during the last century have soundly endorsed the accuracy of the New Testament text, and completely defeated the notions of John's gospel having been written in 150–200 A.D.

Does it shake my faith that we don't have an original? Not at all. The time span between the original and our earliest copies is extremely short. Besides this, our copies are so good and so numerous that it is possible that we would not recognize an original if we had it. Besides if we had the "originals" we would probably worship them instead of live them.

Confirmation of Archaeology

What has happened over the last few centuries has been nothing short of breathtaking in the study of ancient manuscripts of the New Testament. Beginning a few hundred years ago, scholars began to travel the world, visiting monasteries, libraries, and churches. A huge effort was made to find, catalogue, photograph, and preserve the ancient New Testament manuscripts that had come down to us. Rather than prove that the Scriptures were a confused hash of intermingled legends, this effort has encouraged believers around the world by confirming the text, as well as dispelling any doubt in the integrity of the Scriptures. Believe it or not, we now have roughly 5686 ancient Greek manuscripts of the New Testament in libraries, museums, churches, and monasteries around the world. The amount of testimony to the text of the New Testament is almost overwhelming.[19]

Today we have thousands of the "cursive" style

manuscripts from the year 350 A.D. onward. We have hundreds of vellum and parchment manuscripts from 300 A.D. onward. We also have a mountain of papyrus books and fragments from 110 A.D. onward that survive today as well. The papyri have conclusively filled the gap between the originals and the parchment manuscripts from the early fourth century A.D.

Much of the papyri that survive today were found in Egypt. The dry desert climate is conducive to preservation of the paper-like substance. Flinders Petrie, excavating in Central Egypt about 70 miles southwest of Cairo, noticed old sheets of papyrus that were used to wrap some 30 mummies beneath the sand. His find encouraged others.

In 1895, B. P. Grenfell and A. S. Hunt began a systematic search of the region around Oxyrhynchus. They found tens of thousands of documents and fragments. They pulled them from sand-covered rubbish heaps, mummy cases, and even embalmed crocodile bodies. They found letters, bills, receipts, diaries, certificates and almanacs. Some went back to 2000 B.C. Most were of the centuries just before and after Christ. Among them were early Christian writings, priceless pages of Scripture left behind by disciples in the early church. In total they found portions of 27 New Testament manuscripts dating back to the second century A.D. These papyri illustrate just how well the text was copied over the centuries.

Not only did the papyri confirm the text of later

parchment manuscripts, but they also shed some light on the Greek language of the time. There are about 500 words in the New Testament that do not appear in classical Greek, a peculiar vocabulary found only in the Bible. It was a vocabulary that could not have been invented two or three centuries later and inserted into manuscripts spread throughout the ancient world. When these papyri were pulled from the ancient sands, the fragments of the New Testament matched the style and vocabulary of the existing Scriptures, just as one would have expected.

The idea formerly touted by the critics, that the New Testament was written one or two hundred years after the events described took place, is pure rubbish. Few if any dispute the fact that the New Testament books are indeed products of the middle first century.

There is no doubt that the New Testament manuscripts are accurate. The copies that we now have are so early that the small time span between autograph and earliest copy is seen as negligible. Because of the copies we now have there is no doubt that one can read in the Bible the actual words of the authors who wrote the New Testament. As always, you still must decide if you believe the Bible, but it is now generally considered to be the true and accurate transmission of the original text.

Overwhelming Evidence

Christians need to realize the double standard that is often employed today in regard to ancient literature. The New Testament has been put under the microscope, and has come out smelling like a rose. Other ancient books, which scholars accept wholeheartedly, are far weaker in their support. For instance, let us compare the Bible to other well-known works of antiquity. How does the Bible compare to Plato and Aristotle? Extremely well, actually.

Plato wrote in 400 B.C. Our earliest copy dates from 900 A.D. That is a gap of thirteen hundred years! On top of this, there are only seven manuscripts of Plato surviving. Aristotle rests on similarly thin evidence. The gap between the original and our earliest copy is almost fifteen hundred years. And there are only five extant copies surviving. Our earliest copy of the *Odyssey* by Homer dates twenty-two hundred years after the original was supposedly written. Yes, 2,200 years! No one doubts or questions the authenticity of these documents. Scholars universally accept them as accurate transmissions of the ancient text. The Bible is so much better attested that it is almost embarrassing. With most of these other documents, there are gaps of over a thousand years between the original and surviving copies. Not so with the Bible. It was written down shortly after the events occurred, and its copies readily appeared among the early churches.

Table: Comparison of Ancient Writings

Title	Origin	Earliest Copy	Interval	Copies Extant
History of Thucydides	450 BC	900 AD	1350 years	8
Poetics of Aristotle	343 BC	1100 AD	1450 years	5
Caesar's Gallic Wars	50 BC	1000 AD	1050 years	9
Plato	400 BC	900 AD	1300 years	7
Homer's The Iliad	900 BC	400 BC	500 years	643
New Testament	45–80 AD	110 AD	30 years	5686

In comparing the Bible to other ancient written works, one cannot help but notice the sheer number of ancient manuscripts available. The New Testament has between nine times and a thousand times as many surviving manuscripts as the rest. But there is more. Translation of a document was a rare event in the ancient world. We have almost 20,000 copies of the New Testament translated into Latin, Syriac, Coptic, Gothic, Georgian, Ethiopic, and other languages. This pushes the total number of ancient manuscripts to 24,970.[20] Compared to the handful of manuscripts that most ancient documents can boast, the Bible has an astonishing amount of manuscript support a simple fact: The Bible is better attested than the next ten ancient documents combined!

Note this: Anyone who would discard the Bible because of the evidentiary strength of the historical manuscripts would also be forced to discard all of the ancient literature that has come down to us. Such is the strength of the testimony to it.[21]

Of course, the text of the New Testament does not rest alone on the ancient Greek manuscripts and translations. Let this one fact sink in: Even if every single Bible and ancient manuscript fragment of it were burned and destroyed, we would still have virtually the entire New Testament because of the more than 80,000 times it was quoted in the commentaries, sermons, and letters of that period. Only eleven verses would be missing. I personally find this to be very encouraging. While it is wonderful to think of almost 25,000 manuscripts confirming the text of the New Testament, it is also encouraging to have the confirmation of other ancient writers who quoted so early and extensively from the New Testament. These early writers include Clement (96 A.D.), the Didache (100 A.D.), the Epistle of Barnabas (100 A.D.), Ignatius (115 A.D.), and Polycarp (120 A.D.). Even Gnostic heretics like Valentinius (130 A.D.) quoted the Scriptures at length.

Imagine if a fire were to destroy the Constitution of our country. Certainly you would be sad. But would you still know what the original said? Of course. You would still have the exact text because it has been printed and copied into thousands of textbooks and newspapers across the country. The Bible enjoys the same confirmation. Even without any ancient manuscripts, the text could be easily and accurately restored.

Key Points

Allow me to summarize here by listing six concrete reasons to trust that the New Testament has been handed down to us accurately.

1. 24,970 ancient manuscripts. The New Testament is the most thoroughly attested and strongly supported document in all of ancient history. It's better attested than even the next ten ancient documents combined. The evidence for its authenticity is overwhelming. We have thousands of manuscripts from 300 to 1000 A.D. We have papyrus manuscripts and fragments going back to 110 A.D. We have thousands of ancient translations of the Greek text into other ancient languages.[22] This huge body of evidence could not be faked or manufactured. It is, in my opinion, not just strong confirmation of the text of the New Testament. It is concrete proof that the Scriptures we read today have been handed down to us accurately.

2. Written shortly after the events. The New Testament is a collection of eyewitness accounts. It is clear that virtually the entire New Testament was written before 70 A.D.. when the Romans destroyed Jerusalem. The earliest books were written in the 40s, only 15 years after the resurrection of Jesus. The Bible is clearly a product of the middle of the first century, just as it always claimed to be.

3. Thousands of eyewitnesses were still alive. These fervent early critics of christianity would not have allowed inaccuracy. No wild stories and embellished events were added.

4. Libraries of the different regions were in agreement. From Alexandria to Syria, Rome, Carthage, and Constantinople, the manuscripts read virtually the same. In an age without phones or fax machines, this agreement of texts between libraries hundreds of miles apart is a testimony to the accuracy of the Scriptures and confirms the integrity of the text.

5. Quotes from the letters and journals of the time. This fact alone is astounding: Even if every Bible and ancient manuscript were burned today, we would still have the entire New Testament (except eleven verses) because of the 80,000 times it was quoted in the commentaries and letters from that period. Even without any ancient manuscripts or modern Bibles, the text could be easily and accurately restored from the literature of the time.

6. The peculiar nature of Koine Greek. For a long time the New Testament was our only example of *Koine* Greek. Recent discoveries of ancient papyrus fragments have verified its style and vocabulary as authentic. The Koine Greek of the New Testament could not have been faked five or six centuries later. The New Testament is a period piece from the first century.

Our manuscripts are early, accurate, and supported with an overwhelming number of copies. The lines of transmission are completely trustworthy. The New Testament passes all tests for authenticity with flying colors. The last two centuries have produced a wealth of manuscript evidence that has silenced a host of critics. You can read your New Testament and know confidently that you are reading the exact words of the writers. After two centuries of relentless criticism, it is the Bible that has gained respect, while the critics have only been proven to be in error.

Sir Frederic Kenyon, who was the director and principal librarian of the British Museum, and second to none in authority for issuing statements about manuscripts, concludes:

The interval then between the dates of original composition and earliest extant evidence becomes so small as to be in fact negligible, and the last foundation for any doubt that the scriptures have come down to us substantially as they were written has now been removed. Both the authenticity and the general integrity of the books of the New Testament may be regarded as finally established.[23]

I have met Christians who seem almost embarrassed by their simple faith in the accurate transmission of the Scriptures. They have a sheepish grin when they admit that, well, yes, they believe in the Bible, and, yes, they believe it accurately contains the words of the first-century writers. Although many may not realize it, the text of the New Testament has stood like a fortress against all attacks over the last several decades. In fact, rather than crumbling under the weight of criticism, the New Testament stands all the stronger. The weight of the evidence of thousands of ancient manuscripts has firmly come to the support of those who trust the integrity of the Bible.

Christians can be confident in the Scriptures. When you read the New Testament, you are reading the words that the authors penned almost 2000 years ago. There is no need for the disciple to feel embarrassed. Leave that for the critics of decades past. ૐ

CHAPTER FOUR

The Da Vinci Code and 80 Gospels

Dan Brown's book, *The Da Vinci Code*, has now sold 60 million copies worldwide, and has been translated into 44 languages. It puts forward the idea that Jesus and Mary Magdalene married and had children, and that the church hid the truth to this day. Dan Brown wrote his book as complete fiction, but has since converted over (so he says) to the idea that indeed Jesus and Mary were married and had children. According to Brown, at the time of the Crucifixion, Mary was pregnant; after the Crucifixion, she fled to France, where she was sheltered by the Jews of Marseilles; she gave birth to a daughter, named Sarah; the bloodline of Jesus and Mary Magdalene then became the Merovingian dynasty of France, Where their descendants live to this day.

Could this be true? Is there any evidence of this? I for one enjoyed the book. It made for a good mystery. But it was lousy history. *The Da Vinci Code* combines fact and fantasy much like the Indiana Jones series. It's fun, but it's fiction, with just enough truth thrown in to make the plot seem plausible. Brown's ideas have been refuted and rejected time and again by scores of scholars. Yes, there is a *Gospel of Philip* that says that Jesus kissed Mary and that she was his companion.[24] Brown observes that "companion" means "spouse" in Aramaic. It all sounds so convincing when Ian McKellan explains it all on the big screen.

The truth is far simpler. First of all, the *Gospel of Philip* was written about the year 300 A.D., and our earliest copy is approximately a hundred years later. Why should we trust the musings of a Gnostic writer who lived 270 years after the death of Jesus? That is like someone writing a book today proposing that George Washington secretly married Betsy Ross. It makes for an alluring story. But 270 years later, no one will accept it as fact. And that is exactly what happened with the *Gospel of Philip*. Then and now, people who know the background reject the story as obvious fantasy. There is simply no reason to take it seriously.

Second, it is true that "companion" may mean "spouse" in Aramaic. Brown fails to mention, however, that the *Gospel of Philip* exists only in Coptic. There is no proof that it was ever written in Aramaic.

Third, the *Gospel of Philip* was never hidden somewhere and repressed by the Catholic Church. It has been available to the public since it was written. Anyone who takes the time to read and research this "gospel" will see why it has been rejected by every generation of readers.

Did Constantine, who died in 347 A.D., decide which books are in the New Testament as *The Da Vinci Code* claims? No. The books of the Bible had been appearing in lists 200 years before Constantine.[25] *The Da Vinci Code* crumbles upon examination.

One might ask, "But what about the eighty other gospels? How did we end up with only four in the Bible?" Yes, it is true that there are other gospels out there, certainly not eighty. There are gospels of Barnabas, Peter, Thomas, and others. Some of them are only known because they are mentioned by other writers. Manuscripts of others have been discovered. It was not uncommon in ancient times to write under a false name, inventing whimsical stories. These Gnostic gospels were all written at least a hundred years after the life of Jesus and most were written several hundred years later. They were not taken seriously then. Few take them seriously now. In fact, the more you read them, the more you see why the ancients rejected them.

In the *Gospel of Peter* (200 A.D.), Christ comes out of the tomb, with the cross coming out also, moving and talking! In the Acts of John, the apostle John finds bedbugs in his bed at an inn. He commands the bugs to leave and behave themselves! Paul, according to the Acts of Paul, baptizes a lion. Later on his life is saved when he meets up again with the same lion in the arena in Ephesus.

The *Gospel of Thomas* (200 A.D.) is supposed to be secret sayings from Jesus given only to Thomas. At one point Peter is supposed to have told Jesus, "Make Mary leave us, for females don't deserve life." Jesus replies, "Look, I will guide her to make her male, so that she too may become a living spirit resembling you males. For every female who makes herself male will enter the domain of Heaven."

Much like *The Da Vinci Code*, these "Gospels" are interesting reading from the centuries following Jesus. They were not taken seriously in their day, however, and should not be now. On the other hand, the four gospels in our New Testament are there because they are the first-century accounts of the eyewitnesses, either written by the eyewitnesses themselves (Matthew and John), or as a record of the eyewitness accounts (Mark and Luke). *The Da Vinci Code* is like the recent film, *National Treasure.* It may be an entertaining mystery, but it's terrible history. ☙

CHAPTER FIVE

What about Textual Variants?

As discussed earlier, the original autographs of the New Testament have been lost. What we have are copies that have been handed down to us by the churches throughout the centuries. These copies contain errors. Scribes make mistakes. No human hand is so skilled as to be perfect. As some critics are quick to point out, the Greek manuscripts are not in exact agreement. Wording and punctuation differ. How many errors are we discussing? One scholar guessed 200,000 several years ago.[26] A more recent estimate was upwards of 300,000 variants in the text of the New Testament. Yes, you read correctly: 300,000 variants.

Do I accept that number as accurate? Actually, I think it might be a bit low. Does that shake my faith in the

Scriptures? Not at all.

While God inspired the originals, the copies were the work of caring, careful, but still human hands. Although the copyists worked with a zeal for accuracy and precision, they did make occasional mistakes. God did not work a miracle every time a scribe picked up a pen. Mistakes happened.[27]

Those who catalogue textual variants, as these mistakes are called, count *every* variation in *every* Greek manuscript from *every* century, even if the same mistake is repeated in several manuscripts. As there are now almost six thousand ancient Greek manuscripts already catalogued, you can see how the number of variants is going to add up, and as more ancient manuscripts are found and analyzed, the number of variants will continue to grow.

Manuscripts grew up in families. The earlier manuscripts were copied in various cities where the larger churches were located. Rome, Constantinople, Antioch, and Alexandria, for instance, were home to some of the more important libraries. When their manuscripts were copied, mistakes crept in over the centuries. Sometimes a mistake would be carried on down the line. Now, each time that the same mistake is seen, it is counted as another textual variant. Now that we have access to the older manuscripts, textual critics are able to weed out virtually all of the copyists' mistakes.[28]

In practice, these mistakes were usually inconsequential to the meaning of the text. Sometimes words were misspelled. Other mistakes involved word order. A copyist may have read "Jesus Christ" but instead wrote down "Christ Jesus." Sometimes a small word such as "for" or "and" was omitted. Sometimes it was added. Sometimes the scribe would alter the spelling of the word because of the changes in the accepted Greek spelling in his day. (For perspective, just think how much English spelling has changed in the last several hundred years.) By examining the manuscripts and giving weight to the older ones, mistakes like these are easily spotted and corrected. The vast majority of the variants fall into this class.

Looking back, scholars have easily identified mistakes and corrected them. When all is said on the matter, no article of faith is in any way affected by any textual variant. No key scriptures on faith, baptism, salvation, or eternity are remotely affected. No divine command is in question. A quick scanning of the footnotes in your Bible will show you that the text is well established, and rests on solid foundations.

Cambridge scholars B. F. Wescott and F. J. A. Hort were outstanding scholars of the Greek text of the New Testament. They call the great part of textual criticism a work in trivialities. They also stated "the amount of what can in any sense be called substantial variation is but a small fraction of the whole residuary variation, and can hardly form more than a thousandth part of the entire text."[29]

Dr. Douglas Jacoby sums it up: "When a manuscript has a variant, it is compared to other older manuscripts, and a decision is made about which reading is original. In over 99% of these cases, agreement among scholars is total. When it isn't, these trivial variants are indicated in the footnotes of the Bible. What we are saying is that the manuscript variations are *completely insignificant*."[30]

Whatever small variations exist in the text is insignificant. We have the testimony of the eyewitnesses accurately and reliably given to us in the New Testament. It will always be your choice as to whether or not you believe their testimony. Honest seekers, however, will not try to hide behind an imagined cloud of textual problems. The text is accurate, and the New Testament has been transmitted without corruption. Not only does it command our respect and attention, but I also believe it will touch your heart and change your life. ❦

CHAPTER SIX

How Accurate is the Old Testament Text?

The dramatic confirmation that the New Testament has enjoyed over the last few centuries is encouraging. What about the Old Testament? How accurately has its text been preserved?

If you had asked a biblical scholar in 1946 what his dream archeological discovery would be, it would have been to confirm the Old Testament manuscripts. The Jews had worked extremely hard to preserve the text. Painstaking effort and diligence was shown through the ages to ensure the accuracy of each manuscript. They labored to accurately copy their older manuscripts for future readers. They would also destroy copies that became damaged or soiled. After several generations of use in the synagogue, the tattered copy would be carefully copied, then destroyed. They also sent old copies to schools for use there. One way or another, older manuscripts tended to perish in time. They even gave the old manuscripts a ceremonial burial! Such was their deep respect for the Scriptures, as well as for the material upon which was written the sacred name of God.[31]

There developed, therefore, great confidence in the accuracy of the Old Testament text. What was lacking, however, was the concrete evidence that the older texts would have given us. The oldest manuscripts that scholars had to work with were copies dating back to about 900 to 1000 A.D. Were these copies accurate? How garbled had the Old Testament text become? One must remember that the Old Testament had been written over a thousand-year period from 1400 to 400 B.C. (Moses to Malachi). The earliest copies dated back to only 925 A.D. That is a gap of thirteen hundred years. Had the text become corrupted? By the standards of Plato or Aristotle, it was doing just fine. The Old Testament text stood confirmed. Yet just after World War II, dramatic confirmation of the Old Testament text would surface. The greatest archaeological find of the last century would come to be known as *The Dead Sea Scrolls.*

The Discovery of the Century

In 1947, along the border between Israel and Jordan, a Bedouin shepherd was herding his animals near the bottom of a low cliff. There were some caves there, so the young man picked up a stone. Hurling it into one of the caves, he expected to hear it bounce around inside. Instead, he heard the sound of pottery breaking. Being aware of archeological interest in pottery and artifacts, the young man and his friends climbed up to investigate. What they found were some old pottery jars containing ancient scrolls. They brought them to Jerusalem and showed them to various antiquities dealers, as well as archeologists. This sparked a thorough search of the surrounding caves in the area.

In the coming weeks, 200 scrolls and 40,000 inscribed fragments were discovered in eleven different caves. Many of the scrolls were from the Bible. Every Old Testament book was represented in the discovery, except the book of Esther. The other scrolls were religious texts covering a variety of topics. Seemingly by chance, the young shepherd had uncovered the library of the ancient Qumran community outside Jerusalem. Unhappy with the religious practices of their day, the community had retired to the desert, built a settlement, and established their library. It was this library that archeologists were now overjoyed to find.

Quickly it became apparent that the scrolls were far older than anything else available. In fact, the Dead Sea Scrolls are more than a thousand years older than the best Old Testament manuscripts stored in the libraries and museums of Europe and Jerusalem. These new scrolls dated back all the way to 200 B.C. This was a big leap backward in time.

Now the ancient copyists would be tested. How well had the Scriptures been preserved? How accurate had the copyists been? The result: The Jewish Massoretes (textual scholars) had carefully and accurately preserved the Old Testament text. The Dead Sea Scrolls are almost identical to the later manuscripts. While some headlines had predicted that the Bible would have to be rewritten, the result was far more dramatic than that: The ancient scrolls proved that the Bible was was accurately preserved.

How did they manage to so accurately copy the text through the ages? The answer lies in the strict traditions of the Massoretes. Throughout history, during the copying process of a manuscript, if even one letter was missed or added improperly in a new manuscript, the master scribe would destroy the imperfect copy. They were fanatical about accuracy. The Jews had preserved the Old Testament as no other document had ever been preserved. In each manuscript, they actually counted the letters, syllables, words, and paragraphs. Before any manuscript would be accepted, all the letters, syllables, words, and paragraphs would have to be counted and confirmed. Scribes, lawyers, and Massoretes devoted themselves full-time to the accurate transmission of the text. And they were successful.

At Qumran, a scriptorium was discovered. A scriptorium is a room used exclusively for the copying of manuscripts. Shards of pottery upon which the scribes practiced their handwriting were discovered. They would warm up on these scraps of pottery before beginning to copy the manuscripts for their library. Accuracy was an obsession for them. This obsession with accuracy was a part of a long tradition.

For instance, there are almost half a million letters in the first five books of the Old Testament (the Torah). When the Dead Sea Scrolls were studied, they cast doubt on only 169 letters in total from the later copies of the Torah! Amazingly, in almost 500,000 letters, only 169 were questioned. Most were variant spellings or the repetition of a word; no event, practice, or doctrine was affected.

Examination of the Isaiah scroll produced a similar result. After careful study, when the 1952 edition of the Revised Standard Version of the Bible was released, only thirteen very minor changes were made to the text. As Dr. John M. Oakes puts it, "that makes 13 changes to the second longest book in the Old testament over the course of 1000 years."[32]

The scrolls are virtually identical to the Old Testament texts dating from a thousand years later. The scrolls are strong evidence that the Old Testament was accurately preserved. This is just another piece in the jigsaw puzzle, confirming the integrity of the Bible.

As F. F. Bruce stated, "The new evidence confirms what we already had good reason to believe—that the Jewish scribes of the early Christian centuries copied and recopied the text of the Hebrew Bible with utmost fidelity."[33]

Even many skeptical scholars have now been moved to agree that we can trust the historical integrity of the Bible. What we are reading today is an accurate copy of the original. (By the way, the Dead Sea Scrolls give huge weight to the Old Testament messianic prophecies about Jesus, which are now confirmed to have been written centuries *before* Christ.)

Confirmation of our Old Testament is not limited to the Dead Sea Scrolls. Also testifying to the accuracy of the Old Testament text:

• **The Septuagint** (LXX) is a Greek translation of the Hebrew text. Completed in the year 250 B.C., the Septuagint confirms the reliability of the Hebrew text. Tradition has it that 72 elders were sent from Jerusalem to Alexandria, Egypt, in order to help with the translation. It seems the Jewish community in Alexandria was getting a little rusty on their Hebrew, and wanted a copy of the Scriptures in the popular Greek of the day. The elders supposedly completed the task in 72 days. Widely quoted in the New Testament, the Septuagint confirms the reliability of the Hebrew text.

- **First- and second-century writers quote the Old Testament extensively.** Origen retranslated the entire Septuagint; Josephus, Philo and others quoted extensively from the Old Testament. All of this confirms the Old Testament text.

- **The Samaritan Pentateuch** dates to around 400 B.C. It contains the first five books of the Old Testament as preserved by the Samaritans, in a translation of the Pentateuch from Hebrew into Aramaic. Although there are small grammatical differences, the translation gives us an overall confirmation of the first five books of the Old Testament.

- **Aramaic Targums** (commentaries) from 150 A.D. onward quote the Old Testament extensively.

- **A pair of small silver scrolls** (dating from approximately 750 B.C.) was found by archaeologists in 1979 in a tomb in Jerusalem. The scrolls contain an inscription from Numbers 6:24–26. It took three years for the scholars to figure out how to open the scrolls without destroying them. What they discovered was the oldest known copy of any Bible passage. Clearly dated as eighth century B.C., it reads exactly the same as the passage in our modern Bible. It alone has pushed many doubting Thomases to accept that the Old Testament books were indeed written down soon after the events they describe.

We could go on and on. Many books have been written on the reliability of our Biblical text. The main point remains: Rest assured that when you open your Bible, you are reading the text just as it was written. Through the ages, God has seen to it that the Scriptures have come down to us intact. We can confidently open the Bible and know that we are reading the words that the authors penned so many centuries ago.

Again let me quote Sir Frederic Kenyon, former director and principal librarian of the British Museum:

> *"The Christian can take the whole Bible in his hand and say without fear or hesitation that he holds in it the true word of God, handed down without essential loss from generation to generation throughout the centuries."* [34] ☙

END NOTES

1. H. G. Wells, *Outline of History* (Garden City: Garden City Publishing Company, 1931).

2. Will Durant, *Caesar and Christ*. Volume 3 in *The Story of Our Civilization* (New York: Simon & Schuster, 1944).

3. Thallus' original works did not survive but his histories are quoted by a number of early church fathers including Julius Africanus, circa 221 A.D.

4. Tacitus, *The Annals of Imperial Rome*. Revised and translated by Michael Grant (New York: Viking Penguin, Inc., 1971).

5. Gaius Suetonius Tranquillas, *Life of Claudius*, 25.4.

6. Flavius Josephus, *The Antiquities of the Jews*, 93 A.D.

7. British Museum Syriac M.S. Addition 14,658. The date of the manuscript is in the seventh century but the letter itself is from the second or third century.

8. Pliny, *Natural Histories*, 10 volumes in the Loeb Classical Library (Cambridge, MA: Harvard University Press, 1967).

9. *Babylonian Talmud*, Edited by Isidore Epstein (London: The Soncino Press, 1948), Sanhedren 43a.

10. Lucian. *The Death of Peregrine*. In *The works of Lucian of Samosata*, 4 vols. Translated by H. W. Fowler and F. G. Fowler (Oxford: The Clarendon Press, 1949).

11. Study of the tablets and deciphering of the previously unknown Eblaite language is ongoing, and much of the literature on Elba is in archaeological journals and reference books that are probably inaccessible to most readers of this book. For a comprehensive discussion of the general topic, see K. A. Kitchen's *On the Reliability of the Old Testament* (Wm. B. Eerdmans Publishing Co., 2006).

12. The Book of *Revelation* is the one exception. It was written around the year 80 A.D. by the apostle John while exciled on the island of Patmos, near the end of his life.

13. Early papyrus fragments of the New Testament from Egypt date back close to 100 A.D. Some scholars date them even earlier. This conclusively points toward early authorship of the New Testament. Scholars also point to the fact that the destruction of Jerusalem by the Romans in 70 A.D. is not mentioned in the New Testament. Surely this event would have been mentioned if the New Testament dated after 70 A.D. This silence leads many scholars to conclude that the New Testament was completed by 69 A.D. at the latest.

14. John A. T. Robinson, *Redating the New Testament* (Wipf & Stock Publishers, 1976).

15. William F. Albright, *Recent Discoveries in Bible Lands* (New York: Funk and Wagnalls, 1955), 136.

16. William F. Albright, *Christianity Today* (Vol. 7, January 18, 1963), 3.

17. Turtullian, *Ante-Nicene Fathers*, Vols. 3-4, (Peabody, MA: Hendrickson Publishers, 2004).

18. Two spelling variations (i for an ei and an ei for an i), which are of no importance, Considering that Greek spelling, like English spelling today, varies according to regions (e.g., American honor vs. British honour).

19. Focusing on the ancient Greek manuscripts alone, Lightfoot numbers them at 5,686. This number includes 95 papyri, 280 uncials, 2800 miniscules, and 2270 lectionaries. (Uncials are ancient Greek manuscripts written in capital letters on parchment; miniscules are manuscripts written in lower case letters; lectionaries are ancient collections of favorite scripture passages).

20. This large number does not include ostraca, inscriptions, and thousands of early quotations from the New Testament in contemporary literature.

21. Compare this to, say, Buddhism. Buddha's words were not written down until five hundred years after his death. The Hindu Vedas (1500–1200 B.C.) were not written down for seven hundred years. The earliest surviving copy dates back only to 1300 A.D. That's a gap of almost two thousand years between the original and earliest copy.

22. There are approximately ten thousand copies of the New Testament translated into Latin alone.

23. Frederic Kenyon, *The Bible and Archaeology* (London: George G. Harrap & Co., 1940), 288.

24. Darrell L. Bock, Ph.D., *Breaking The Da Vinci Code* (Nashville: Thomas Nelson, Inc., 2004). I highly recommend this book for a thorough analysis of the errors and misrepresentations found in *The Da Vinci Code*.

25. In his book *The Canon of the New Testament*, Princeton New Testament scholar Bruce Metzger details the canonization of scripture. In 367 A.D.

Athanasius was the first to list the twenty-seven books of the New Testament as they exist in most Christian circles. This list came decades after the council of Nicea (325 A.D.), yet this collection process shows that by the end of the second century, the four gospels had become the primary sources of Jesus' life and ministry.

26. Neil R. Lightfoot, *How We Got the Bible*, Second Edition (Grand Rapids, Mich: Baker Book House, 1993), 67.

27. While our focus here is on variants in the Greek text, it is interesting to note that mistakes have also been made in the English text after it was properly translated. The first edition of the King James Bible had more than two hundred mistakes, and had to be reprinted two years later. Editions of various English bibles from the 20th century had printing errors that were caught later.

28. For instance, if the scribe reads "Jesus arrived at Capurnaum," but copies "Jesus arrived in Capurnaum," then we would have a textual variant. If 150 other scribes copy his mistake in the years to come, then all 150 mistakes would be catalogued as variants, even though it is the same mistake. At first, 200,000 variants is a scary thought. When you realize that those variants are the total contained in almost 6,000 Greek manuscripts, you understand just how accurate the text is.

29. B. F. Westcott and F. J. A. Hort,, *The New Testament in the Original Greek* (New York: The Macmillan Company, 1946).

30. Douglas Jacoby, *True and Reasonable: Reasons for Belief in an Age of Doubt* (Spring, Texas:, Illumination Publishers, 2005), 68.

31. Neil R. Lightfoot, *How We Got the Bible*, Second Edition (Grand Rapids, Mich: Baker Book House, 1993), 90.

32. John M. Oakes, *Reasons For Belief: A Handbook of Christian Evidence* (Spring, Texas: Illumination Publishers, 2006), 161.

33. F. F. Bruce, *Second Thoughts on the Dead Sea Scrolls* (Eerdmans Publishing Co., 1956), 61–62.

34. Sir Frederick Kenyon. *Our Bible and the Ancient Manuscripts.* Revised by A. W. Adams (Harper and Brothers, 1958), 55.

FURTHER READING

Aland, Kurt, and Barbara Aland, *The Text of the New Testament: An Introduction to the Critical Editions and to the Theory and Practice of Modern Textual Criticism.* Second revised edition. Grand Rapids, Mich.: William B. Eerdmans Publishing Co., 1995.

Ankerberg, John, and John Weldon, *Ready with an Answer.* Eugene, Ore.: Harvest House, 1997.

Archer, Gleason, *A Survey of Old Testament Introduction. Revised edition*, updated by Dillon Burroughs. Chicago: Moody Publishers, 2007.

Bock, Darrell L., *Breaking The Da Vinci Code.* Nashville, Tenn.: Thomas Nelson, Inc., 2004.

Bruce, F. F., *The New Testament Documents: Are They Reliable?* Downers Grove, Ill.: InterVarsity Press, 1943. Reprinted 2001.

Comfort, Philip Wesley, *Essential Guide to Bible Versions.* Revised expanded version. Carol Stream, Ill.: Tyndale House, 2000.

Comfort, Philip Wesley, *The Origin of the Bible.* Wheaton, IL: Tyndale House Publishers, 1992.

Ehrman, Bart D., *The New Testament: A Historical Introduction to the Early Christian Writings.* New York: Oxford University Press, 2000.

Evans, Craig A., *Fabricating Jesus: How Modern Scholars Distort the Gospels.* Downers Grove, Ill.: InterVarsity Press, 2006.

Jacoby, Douglas, *True and Reasonable: Reasons for Faith in an Age of Doubt.* Spring, Texas: Illumination Publishers, 2005.

Kinnard, Steve, *Getting the Most from the Bible.* Woburn, Mass.: Discipleship Publications Intl., 2000.

Lightfoot, Neil R., *How We Got the Bible.* Third Edition. New York: MJF Books, 2003.

McDowell, Josh, *The New Evidence That Demands a Verdict.* Nashville, Tenn.: Thomas Nelson, 1999.

McGrath, Alister, *In the Beginning: The Story of the King James Bible and How It Changed a Nation, a Language, and a Culture.* New York: Random House, Inc., 2001.

Metzger, Bruce, *The Canon of the New Testament: Its Origin, Development, and Significance.* Oxford: Clarendon, 1987.

Metzger, Bruce, and Bart D. Ehrman. *The Text of the New Testament: Its Transmission, Corruption, and Restoration.* Fourth edition. New York: Oxford: Oxford University Press, 2005.

Oakes, John M., *Reasons for Belief. A Handbook of Christian Evidence.* Spring, Texas: Illumination Publishers, 2005.

Scanlin, Harold, *The Dead Sea Scrolls and Modern Translations of the Old Testament.* Carol Stream, Ill.: Tyndale House Publishers, 1993.

Wegner, Paul D., *The Jouney from Texts to Translations.* Grand Rapids, Mich: Baker Academic, 1999.

Mike Taliaferro

Born in Texas, raised in Virginia, Mike graduated from Abilene Christian University in 1981 with a bachelors degree in Bible. Mike and Anne-Brigitte married in 1981, and moved to Boston and then New York to help plant a church there in 1983. The Taliaferro's went on to plant and lead churches in Sao Paulo, Brazil (1987), Abidjan, Ivory Coast (1989), Nairobi, Kenya (1991), and then moved to South Africa where they worked for over a decade leading the Johannesburg Church of Christ.

The Taliaferros moved to San Antonio, Texas, in 2003, where they currently serve the Mission Point Christian Church as Lead Evangelist and Women's Ministry Leader. Mike has over a quarter million books in print, and has visited more than 50 countries. Also Mike Taliaferro, along with Justin Renton serve as editors at **www.icochotnews.com**.

Contact: mtaliaferro1@satx.rr.com

Additional Teaching Material by Mike Taliaferro

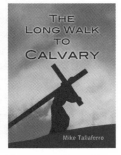

The Killer Within
ISBN: 1-5778204-2-8
134 pgs. Paperback
Price: $10.00

The Lion Never Sleeps
ISBN: 1-57782-184-X
88 pgs. Paperback
Price: $11.00

The Long Walk to Calvary
ISBN: 978-0-9824085-6-8
9 messages on 2 MP3 CDs
Price: $10.00

Available at www.ipibooks.com